PSALM 139

Hope and Healing
For Abortion Recovery

LORNA R. CARRARA

Website: www.lornacarrara.com
Facebook: Yourpsalm139
Email: yourpsalm139@gmail.com

PSALM 139

Hope and Healing
For Abortion Recovery

Endorsements

Fellow Psalm 139'rs... there is no greater grief than to have ended another person's life by choice, either because of inconvenience or just not wanting the child. The challenge that is never calculated is what you have done to yourself inside, the thoughts of guilt, shame, and even suicide. I have known Lorna for over 30 Years, and can personally attest to the verity of every word penned on these pages. Lorna has skillfully put down in print the feelings and needs of those who are survivors of abortion. May you find the freedom you so greatly need… Psalm 139 is a book in which you will learn the freedom that is offered by the suffering Savior… may the Lord shine the bright light of His salvation upon every dark corner of your life.

— **Dr. Robb Thompson,**
Founder Of Family Harvest Church,
Author, Speaker & Mentor.

I have known Lorna for over 20 years. She is a woman who speaks from the heart. Not only has Lorna experienced what she has written, but lives out her freedom in Christ. Today she is sharing it so others can experience what she has. I know you will be ministered to as you read and act upon the wisdom she offers from God's word.

— **Linda Thompson,**
Author, Founder of Bella Women's Group,
Displaying Acts of Kindness & Caring for Children In Need.

There's never been a generation that needs this book more than this one. If you've experienced abortion or were part of an abortion decision, this book and complimentary study guide will help to bring you freedom and saturate your spirit with God's incredible love! Through the powerful Biblical scriptures in Psalm 139, you will join the ranks of those who are desperate for forgiveness from the Lover of our souls!

– Scott Kemp
Celebrate Recovery™ Regional Director

Having known Lorna for 10 years, it is evident that in-spite of the situations she has faced, her spirit has been revived and she is radiant! The principles in this book will not only help in abortion recovery but also provide relief to many people experiencing emotional pain from the challenges in their lives.

– Malachi Kelly, MAPC
Mental Health Therapist

Lorna came to speak to our Celebrate Recovery™. She spoke with passion, conviction and grace as she shared her personal journey of healing from abortion. She conveyed the harsh reality that abortion is sin without sugar coating it but at the same time weaved a tapestry of grace and love throughout her message of hope. The love of Jesus has obviously taken up residence in Lorna and His Spirit moves powerfully through her!

– Jeff & Deb Price,
Celebrate Recovery™ Ministry Leaders,
Kalamazoo MI.

"Lorna came and shared her amazing post-abortion recovery journey during our Celebrate Recovery™ meeting at Hope Church. Her testimony, combined with insightful truths from Psalms 139 brought release, freedom, and joy to men and women. Many people have been indirectly affected by the pain, guilt, and sorrow of abortion. One attendee stated that she realized "her only future niece had been aborted." This message brings truth, comfort, and healing."

— Bruce and Sandy Stefanich,
Celebrate Recovery™ Ministry Leaders - Hope Church,
LaGrange, IL.

Thank you for sharing your message with us. You did an amazing job and I know God is using you to raise people's awareness about the destructive aftermath of abortion.

– J.P.,
IL.

Thank you for opening my eyes in realizing that I'm not alone. The freedom of being able to confess is the first step toward healing. Thank you again for sharing your message and also for being so open and honest with your own experience!

– D.G.,
IL.

CONTENTS

Dedication

To you: The one who is holding this book. I have prayed for your courage to throw open this closet door and face what seeks to remain hidden. God loves you. It was never His plan that you would suffer guilt, shame and fear. He is waiting for you to receive His forgiveness. It's only a prayer away.

My loving husband, Steve. You are my greatest example of Integrity, Strength, Courage and Character. Without your pure unconditional love and constant support, I could never be who I am, nor go where my road is taking me. You give me the courage and strength to step out onto these waters. I love you with everything I am.

Acknowledgements

Pastors Robb and Linda Thompson, my Pastors and mentors for 30+ years. Thank you for teaching me the Word of God, for showing me what Dedication, Excellence, Generosity and Unconditional Love look like by continually living it in front of me all these years. Your life's sacrifice reaches farther than you could ever know. I love you both with my heart.

Celebrate Recovery Ministries™, Celebrate Recovery™ helped me find myself again. By attending CR, I found the strength to start talking about my life, to connect the dots from the present to my past and let God use it all. He took my mess and made a message! Thank you Celebrate Recovery™.

Special thanks to:

Cherise Nicole Ragland of CN Media for your help, instruction, and creative ideas. Put a baby in the 9? Brilliant!

Sarah Loehr – The Sarah Co. Graphic & Print – Thank you for creating the logo, creating my advertising copy and designing the covers for both books! You put a picture to my dream.

Tom Nestor – Speaker/Author/Founder of Leadership Today – Your knowledge and direction has been so valuable to me. Thank you for helping me navigate through the publication process and beyond. God has such a plan for you, thank you.

My friends Jane Jarosz and Patty Plante: your continued encouragement and cheerleading gave me strength and courage. Thank you for loving me and being my friends.

Introduction

This is a beautiful message from our loving Heavenly Father, to those who are suffering from the result of an abortion decision. If abortion has touched your life somehow, this book will be very beneficial to you, and even life-changing. God has a powerful message to those who are hurting, suffering, stuck, and broken. God wants you to understand that He knows, He was there, and He forgives. He will also show you how to do the same!

Why am I writing this book? Well, to be sincere, an Abortion Recovery Ministry is not what I had envisioned for my future. I love to sing in my church, attend small groups, and even lead now and then, but to go out into the world and talk about abortion to strangers? Then to shine a spotlight on the very thing they want to hide forever because everyone is going to point fingers at them? Not to mention it would be shining a spotlight on my life and it would shine directly on the things I don't care to talk about. No, that was not my dream! However, I sensed God leading me in this direction, and in studying Psalm 139, I began to get a greater revelation of His love for us. I felt His longing for His children that are bound in this and it drove me to share this message. I wrote it out and began sharing it with groups all over Illinois and Michigan. Then one day I got an email from a woman who wrote: "I couldn't come that night to hear you, but my friends there told me about your message. My daughter has had an abortion and is withdrawing from everything: friends, youth group, and church. She seems broken somehow. Is there some way I can get this message for her?"

Unfortunately, there wasn't, and it broke my heart! I wanted to help her, and therefore the message became a book. It also became a 10-week small group study for anyone who wants to get deeper into the message of Psalm 139 and heal from an abortion decision. You can find healing whether it is from your abortion or someone else's abortion that has touched your life. I am very excited about this book because I know it will bring healing, freedom, joy, and peace. For me, the bottom line is this: I love people, and I love to help people. God has taken me from such a dark place, poured out His amazing love onto my life and healed me. The Bible says in **2 Corinthians 1:4 "He comforts us in all our troubles so that we can *comfort* others. When they are troubled, we will be able to give them the *same comfort* God has given us."**

So, I must go! I must write this and tell you so that you can receive healing. Then you can tell others about His Psalm of healing, love, and forgiveness. Abortion is an incredibly

painful topic for so many. It is worse than punching a bruise. It can be like twisting a knife right inside your heart. I know, because I was one of those, but God has put this message in my heart and made it clear to me that He wants it to reach the hurting far and wide. As far and wide as I can reach, it will go. It is a message of ownership, repentance, forgiveness, and above it all, to coin a lyric, the "overwhelming, never-ending reckless love of God." It is the beautiful love story of how He pursues us, chases after us, whispers love to us and woos us to Him. Oh, the precious love of God! He is coming after the ones who think He has forgotten them. The broken, hiding in shame pretending everything's ok. You know it's not, and so does He. He longs for you, for things to be right between you and Him. That is the reason for this book. And let me say: Even if abortion hasn't touched your life in a personal way, maybe it has damaged someone you love, or you may be reading this with a desire to know how to help someone who can't speak for themselves. Whatever your reason I'm so glad you here! So settle in and read on, and I promise you will never be the same.

CHAPTER 1

Before I Knew Him,
He Knew Me

As I begin to share the message with you, I'd like to tell you a little about myself, so you know where I'm coming from, and why it's me that writing this book. I was where you are. I had an abortion in 1983. It was the only child I ever would have had. But let me back up a bit. I grew up in a small town in Illinois in the '70s. My childhood was terrific. It was filled with love, laughter, great family, music, good food, and culture, until the bottom fell out one night in May 1971. My wonderful mother who was so full of life fell unconscious and was taken away by ambulance while I slept. I awoke to find her gone, and she never came home. Three days later she died of a massive brain hemorrhage. She was only 46 years old, and I was only 11. Everything I was, who I was, truly ended on that fateful night. My life would never be the same. For years following, my father, brother and I stumbled along, going through the motions of life, laughing but not happy. We were numb to everything happening around us. We separated from each other emotionally just because none of us knew how to live together without her. She was life itself. Everyone loved my mother. Those childhood years and many following are still a blur to me. I really don't have many childhood memories and certainly not many good ones. Her death created such a cavern of loss. Affection, attention, loving words, caring touch, were now gone. We were all just getting through life. It was as if love was gone. I don't have any memories of my father or brother ever telling me that they loved me. I knew they did, but there was such an abyss of tangible love lost in all our lives at the time.

I wasn't getting what I needed at home, and I was getting older. Boys started paying attention to me. I found that I could have the feelings of love and acceptance from boys. So, I began trading my innocence and my moral standards for that perception of "love and acceptance." My house was empty all the time. My father stayed at work, and my brother was in college. Unfortunately, the kind of kids who would want to hang around in an empty house started hanging around with me. Since it was the 70's drugs were everywhere. Then as I grew older my Jr. High and High School days were filled with pot smoking and pill popping kids. You could get anything you wanted anywhere. I started experimenting and playing around with different sources to numb my pain, but

I began trading my innocence and my moral standards for that perception of "love and acceptance

nothing ever really made the hurt go away. I was so lonely and insecure. I must have acted needy because I kept getting rejected by boy after boy, and then man after man.

As life went on the drugs and alcohol became more sophisticated. Beer and pot changed to Wine, Tequila, and Cocaine. I was drinking regularly and was well on my way to becoming an alcoholic. I was the best arm candy, party girl, and life of the party! However, I still couldn't understand why no one would love me forever? What

> *It wasn't real to me, just a positive test, and not a baby*

was I doing wrong? Then in 1983, I became pregnant. I couldn't even believe it. It wasn't real to me, just a positive test, and not a baby. I can honestly say that none of my friends or anyone I can remember encouraged me to keep it, to have the baby. They all told me to get an abortion. They said, "You're too young for kids. You need to have them later when you settle down." I don't even remember considering keeping it. Back then there was not the technology we have available today with ultrasounds and pregnancy centers. I knew from friends that I just had to go to the clinic and be convincing that this was what I wanted, and it would all be over. Then I could get back to my "lifestyle." My boyfriend was more than willing to pay for it, so I made an appointment to have it done and get on with life, so I thought.

I can remember vividly being on that table. The doctor was cold and uncaring, while the nurse held my hand. There were no drugs. The nurse told me just to hang on and squeeze her hand until it was over. It was horrible. The pain from the doctor inserting the rods, forcing my tight safe womb open against its will. I knew the very moment my child's life was pulled from me, and the exact moment the separation happened because I felt it. I knew in that *instant* that I had done something terribly wrong. As soon as he took my baby's life, the guilt came in like *a flood*. And the remorse! I cried immediately and couldn't stop. They took me into a room that had beds on the floor, and I lay on one and cried and cried. After 15 minutes they made me get up off the floor, sit and have some cookies and juice because I was so dizzy. I sat there staring at the table in front of me feeling dead inside. After a few minutes, they told me I had to go. I remember praying that there would not be any of those

> *Little did I know, I had just taken the life of the only child I ever would have had*

"sign holder fanatics" outside when I left. I wouldn't have been able to handle that. I never felt lonelier than at that moment. Little did I know, I had just taken the life of the only child I ever would have had.

CHAPTER 2

How I Met Him

I went on with life, stuffing the pain, the guilt, and leaving it all in a dark corner of my mind. I refused to acknowledge it or ever look at it again. After a time, I began searching for a greater understanding of God. I had been raised to believe, to know who HE was, but I had no idea He was interested in knowing and having a relationship with *me*. I thought He was far too busy and had too many things to keep track of to be bothered with the sorry likes of me. Oh, how wrong I was! In 1986 I had a roommate who had just become a Christian. She began going to Bible Studies after work, and she was so happy! I wanted whatever she was getting at these Bible Studies. I was getting to a point where I knew there was more than what I knew about God; I just didn't know how to find it. I asked her if I could go with her to a Bible Study, and she ended up having one in our home. I attended, and in listening to the man named Tom that was leading it, I began to hear things I had never heard before. He shared with me

> **John 3:16: "For this is how much God loved the world—he gave his one and only, unique Son as a gift. So now everyone who believes in him will never perish but experience everlasting life." (TPT)**

He began to explain this love to me. He showed me

> **Romans 3:23: "For we all have sinned and are in need of the glory of God." (TPT)**

And

> **Romans 5:8: "But Christ proved God's passionate love for us by dying in our place while we were still lost and ungodly!" (TPT)**

I was certainly ungodly. I was so ashamed of all the things I had done, and I couldn't even think about the abortion. I couldn't believe He would want me. I was so lost and in so much sin. The scriptures Tom was showing me seemed to speak right to me, right into my life where I was at that exact moment. He showed me:

Titus 3:3-7: "Once we, too, were foolish and disobedient. We were misled and became slaves to many lusts and pleasures. Our lives were full of evil and envy, and we hated each other. But when God our Savior revealed His kindness and love, He saved us, not because of the righteous things we had done, but because of His mercy. He washed away our sins, giving us a new birth and new life through the Holy Spirit. He generously poured out the Spirit upon us through Jesus Christ our Savior. Because of His grace, he made us right in his sight and gave us confidence that we will inherit eternal life." (NLT)

I had no idea I could wash away my past. I thought my horrible sins and my abortion were too high on the list.

Tom said that Jesus died for me and shed his blood as a sacrifice for everyone, and that included me! He even went so far as to say that Jesus would have done it all, even if only for me. If I was the only one left on earth, he would do it to get me back! His blood was shed for *me*. For *me*! He told me that God *knew* me, really cared about me, and not only cared

> *He even went so far as to say that Jesus would have done it all, even if only for me*

about me but *loved* me! It was all so beautiful yet so hard to understand. He showed me many scriptures about the amazing unconditional love of God. Then I asked him the question that had been keeping me from God all these years. The lie that I had been believing, and not knowing any better: I said, "What you're telling me is so wonderful! I want to believe it, but if this is true why would such a loving God take a mother from a young girl and leave me so scared and so alone?" (I never thought God cared anything about me. Have you ever felt that way? I believed in life this was just the way the cards fell. If you're lucky, you get a mom, if not you're me.) Tom just smiled and told me that God would have never taken her from me, He loved her too. He explained that sickness is not from Him and that I have an enemy. The devil deceived Adam and Eve, and their sin brought a curse into the world. The devil is the author of sickness and disease. And there are also now circumstances of life, genetics, signs my mother may have ignored, but in all this, God LOVED me more than I could ever imagine, and He would *never* hurt me. I began to think about the horrendous headaches my mother used to have and all the pressure she had put herself under, many times against my father's wishes, and it began to make sense. I don't know why all of that happened, but it brought me hope knowing that God wasn't behind it. He loves me! He wasn't making me pay for something, or just in general not caring about me. When I realized that God loved me, had a plan for me and most of all wanted a relationship with me, my heart soared! It was like not having any friends, and then the President of the United States came to me and wanted to be my best friend! I felt like someone

> *God LOVED me more than I could ever imagine, and He would **never** hurt me*

8

that mattered for the first time in so many years. GOD cared about me and what happened to me! Tom then showed me

> **Romans 10: 9-10: "If you openly declare that Jesus is Lord and believe in your heart that God raised him from the dead, you will be saved. For it is by believing in your heart that you are made right with God, and it is by openly declaring your faith that you are saved." (NLT)**

I received Jesus as my Lord and Savior that night, and I have never looked back. My life has never been the same. My heart was flooded with the love of God. Filled to overflowing with His loving-kindness, peace, and contentment. I found out that I am now a "new creation":

> **2 Corinthians 5:17: Now, if anyone is enfolded into Christ, he has become an entirely new creation. All that is related to the old order has vanished. Behold, everything is fresh and new. (TPT)**

I want to take a moment here to invite you to do what I did and have what I and millions of others now have! The Bible says that God is no respecter of people. He loves us all the same. If you have never asked Jesus to have rule over your life, to be your personal Lord and Savior (and best friend anyone could ever have, I promise) you can do it right now! Pray this from your heart:

Lord Jesus, I see how I need you. Come into my life, flood my heart with your love. I ask you to forgive me of all my sins, wash me clean and make me new. Be the Lord of my life right now. In Jesus name, Amen.

Praise God! If you just prayed that for the first time, let me know so I can celebrate with you! You can reach me at *Yourpsalm139* on Facebook or email me at *yourpsalm139@gmail.com* I really want to know! I will personally welcome you into the wonderful family of believers all over the world just like you. If you don't tell me, tell someone, and get into a good church where they teach the Bible. I promise you will never regret it and you'll never be the same.

Now that I was a Christian, I began studying the Bible like Jesus was coming back next week. I was ravenous, and couldn't get enough. I learned all about being free from fear, living free from sickness and disease, I studied about the love of God, and the blood covenant, on and on. I knew I was forgiven, washed and made clean. The drug habit fell off, the smoking habit fell off, then fear, anger, and insecurities, but I didn't talk to anyone (or God) about the abortion. It remained in me as an unconfessed sin… quiet, waiting. I didn't want to look at it. It was such an incredibly painful experience. I just wanted to leave it and hoped it would fade into oblivion. I was forgiven, wasn't

I? I would be so indignant when many Christians would point fingers at those people who had abortions. How did they know about me? How could they judge me? I had a wave of anger whenever I approached the subject, or anyone else brought it up. I refused to talk about it. Technically I was forgiven. Yes, God forgives all sin, but we still need to repent and ask for forgiveness. We need to tell Him we understand and what we did was wrong. He is faithful to forgive, but we must ask. Well, I hadn't asked for forgiveness for it yet and, unfortunately, it was really holding me back. God wanted me to deal with this. So, He put me in the right place at the right time.

I was forgiven, washed and made clean

CHAPTER 3

The Day He Opened my Eyes

One weekend I was at an outdoor Jesus conference. It was a weekend of tent meetings, current Christian music concerts, and general teaching sessions on various topics. On the 2nd day, I attended a tent meeting where the speaker was talking about the pro-life agenda, and "those people" who had abortions. I was so mad I left the meeting! It seemed like everywhere the topic came up, I heard about "those women." Well, I was one of "those women" and what did people know about me? I was so angry at the judgement. I went walking through a grassy field looking for another meeting that wouldn't smack me so hard. To me this was beyond punching a bruise, it was twisting a knife in me. Someone had to understand where I was at mentally at the time, there had to be grace here! Suddenly it was as if the Holy Spirit opened my eyes and I saw what I had done! I saw abortion as murder. It was as if a veil was lifted from my eyes, and someone blew the clouds away, and I saw how God felt about abortion. "Oh GOD" I cried! "What have I done?" "What did I do?" "Oh Father, I didn't know." "I really didn't know!" That was all I could say. I hadn't seen it so clearly until then. Honestly, I believe one of the hardest parts of abortion recovery is the fact that abortion is legal! *I thought because it was legal it was ok!* Let me make something very clear here in case you are still wondering. In Gods eyes, abortion is NOT ok. It's murder. Thou shalt not kill is the 6th commandment.

But... He is God...and there is grace and forgiveness.

I literally fell to the ground and cried for a very long time that day. I kept saying "what have I done, what have I done?" The pain, hurt, anger and frustration came pouring out along with the remorse for what I had done. God

> *I thought because it was legal it was ok!*

in His infinite love and rich mercy chose such a wonderful place for me to be when the Holy Spirit gently revealed to me my unconfessed sin. As it turned out the theme of this conference was Pro-life!

I was surrounded by people who understood my pain. After a while, as I got myself together, I got up and found another meeting where a woman was explaining how to deal with Post-Abortion Syndrome (PAS). This was a Christian conference, so I received scripture and prayer to help me immediately. God is so good. After that conference, I found an abortion recovery program. Through that program, I received forgiveness, forgave, and most of all I forgave myself.

Fast forward 30+ years, I have been singing in my church, I released a CD a few years ago, my husband and I were ministry leaders for a recovery ministry (Celebrate Recovery™) in our church, I wasn't really thinking about a new career path at all. I figured for the next 30+ years I'd stay in music. I had dealt with my abortion many years previous, I was healed of the pain guilt and shame, and was ministering to women in the recovery ministry and in church on post-abortion recovery. I was helping them or someone they knew deal with the aftermath of abortion. During this time my husband and I were camping one weekend in the forests of Wisconsin.

God in His infinite love and rich mercy chose such a wonderful place for me to be when the Holy Spirit gently revealed to me my unconfessed sin

I was up very early having my wonderful bible time, sitting drinking my coffee, listening to the wind sing through the pines, and reading Psalm 139. When suddenly it was as if God blew the clouds away again. As I read this Psalm, it was like reading a beautiful love letter from Him to all His precious girls. I sat in awe at what I was reading, a Psalm I had read so many times before, but now it was all new. It was for you my friend, whoever you are. The one who is searching for hope, healing, and forgiveness from abortion. If you have had an abortion, or know someone who has, if you have paid for someone to have an abortion, if it has touched you in any way, you must read what God is saying to you. Every time I minister this message, I sense such a longing in my heart, the Father longing for his children. He wants you free from the guilt and shame that is covering you like a shroud. He paid the ultimate price anyone could pay for your freedom, and He wants you free to laugh, dance, sing and rejoice in His amazing love for you. Let me show you the way through this Psalm.

CHAPTER **4**

The Psalm/The Message

Psalm 139 (NLT)

¹ O Lord, you have examined my heart
and know everything about me.
² You know when I sit down or stand up.
You know my thoughts even when I'm far away.
³ You see me when I travel
and when I rest at home.
You know everything I do.
⁴ You know what I am going to say
even before I say it, Lord.
⁵ You go before me and follow me.
You place your hand of blessing on my head.
⁶ Such knowledge is too wonderful for me,
too great for me to understand!

[7] I can never escape from your Spirit!

    I can never get away from your presence!

[8] If I go up to heaven, you are there;

    if I go down to the grave, you are there.

[9] If I ride the wings of the morning,

    if I dwell by the farthest oceans,

[10] even there your hand will guide me,

    and your strength will support me.

[11] I could ask the darkness to hide me

    and the light around me to become night—

[12] but even in darkness I cannot hide from you.

    To you the night shines as bright as day.

    Darkness and light are the same to you.

[13] You made all the delicate, inner parts of my body

    and knit me together in my mother's womb.

[14] Thank you for making me so wonderfully complex!

    Your workmanship is marvelous—how well I know it.

[15] You watched me as I was being formed in utter seclusion,

    as I was woven together in the dark of the womb.

[16] You saw me before I was born.

    Every day of my life was recorded in your book.

    Every moment was laid out

    before a single day had passed.

[17] How precious are your thoughts about me, O God.

    They cannot be numbered!

[18] I can't even count them;

they outnumber the grains of sand!

And when I wake up,

you are still with me!

[19] O God, if only you would destroy the wicked!

Get out of my life, you murderers!

[20] They blaspheme you;

your enemies misuse your name.

[21] O Lord, shouldn't I hate those who hate you?

Shouldn't I despise those who oppose you?

[22] Yes, I hate them with total hatred,

for your enemies are my enemies.

[23] Search me, O God, and know my heart;

test me and know my anxious thoughts.

[24] Point out anything in me that offends you,

and lead me along the path of everlasting life.

CHAPTER **5**

He Was There

¹ O Lord you have examined my heart and
   know everything about me.
² You know when I sit down or stand up. You
   know my thoughts even when I'm far away.
³ You chart the path ahead of me and tell me
   where to stop and rest. Every moment you
   know where I am.
⁴ You know what I am going to say even before
   I say it, Lord.
⁵ You go before me and follow me, you place
   your hand of blessing on my head.
⁶ such knowledge is too wonderful for me, too
   great for me to understand!

In this part of the Psalm God is explaining how well he knows you. Better than your closest friend, brother or sister. Better than your parents know you, your closest coworker or even your spouse! God *knows* you intimately. He knows everything about you. He knows you better than you know yourself! He formed you. He made you, He created you. He gave you your first breath. He knows you inside and out, everything about you. Everywhere

> *He formed you. He made you, He created you. He gave you your first breath*

you've *ever* been, anything you've *ever* done since you were in your mother's womb. *Every* thought you have *ever* had! Even when you were a child. He knows you and the intents of your heart. All the things you say under your breath, mumble or just think in your mind, He knows. He knows what you're going to do next. He is trying to get us to understand that He *knows* us and knows what we're doing and still loves us! More than we could ever think! But He wants you to realize that everything you've ever done, He's been with you when you did it. *Everything.* Even if He does not have entrance into your heart because you have not invited Him in yet, He is still with you everywhere you are. The Bible says in Mathew 5:45 "He rains over the just and the unjust," you cannot hide from Him. He has been with us and is still, everywhere. This is so hard for us to even think about, hard to understand, no one knows us that well! But God does. He was with you in the womb. He was there the first time you fell, he saw your first tears, and your most recent, you can just stop right here and ponder that for a little while to get an understanding of how intimately He knows us. I know we don't think about that so much, but He does. We never leave His sight or thoughts. I realize this knowledge can bring comfort or conviction depending on where you're at right now, and I understand. But in all of it, please never forget, He WAS there and saw and felt all of it with you, and still desperately loves you, you are *so* precious to him.

> ⁷ I can *never* escape from your Spirit! I can
> *never* get away from your presence!
> ⁸ If I go up to heaven, you are there:
> if I go down to the *place of the dead* you
> are there.

If you're in a good place with God, this will bring you comfort, that we can never escape His spirit. I don't ever want to be without the Holy Spirit as my comfort and guide. But, if you've had an abortion, this section, particularly verse 8 might be hard for you to hear. He was with us everywhere we have ever been, and He always will be with us. When you had your abortion, He was there with you, *in the place of the dead.* That may be the clinic, hospital, wherever you had

> *He WAS there and saw and felt all of it with you, and still desperately loves you, you are so precious to him*

your abortion. He was there. He was with you. That is hard to think about, but it helps us come out of hiding when we realize He was there watching. His heart was breaking as yours was. He knows. He held *you* as the nurse held your hand, He is everywhere a life begins and ends because He is life. He is creation. I'm not saying He was pleased, or it was ok with Him that you were getting an abortion, I'm merely pointing out where in verse 8 says He was there. It is important for you to know that.

> ⁹ If I ride the wings of the morning, if I dwell
>   by the farthest oceans
> ¹⁰ Even there your hand will guide me, your
>   strength will support me.
> ¹¹ I could ask the darkness to hide me and the
>   light around me to become as night.
> ¹² But even in darkness I cannot hide from you.
>   To you the night shines as bright as day.
>   Darkness and light are both alike to you.

We cannot hide from Him. At the bottom of the sea, he's there. (I can attest to that as a scuba diver, I sense His presence as He shows me the wonders of the deep all the time.) In the darkness, he is there. Darkness is as light to him. We cannot hide. So why try? He is saying "come to me, you cannot hide. I see your heart. I know you. I can help you, and I understand."

Think about when your child or someone you know does something wrong and you know about it, don't you want to tell them "I saw what you did, I know, let's talk about it."

Don't run and hide. There is no hiding, He's everywhere, and He loves you. He knows, and He loves you. He went through it with you, and He still loves you, because He loves YOU. Not because of what you DO. Not because you act right or say the right things. He can't do anything else, because He is love. He loved me when I had my abortion and years later when I could handle it, He gently showed me how wrong it was.

He waited until I could take the pain it was going to bring. He knew when I could/would repent and make it right with Him. That's what He is concerned about with us. He is concerned with making everything right. Our repentance, for us to receive the precious blood of Jesus as atonement for our sin and run back to the Him for a relationship. That's what He longs for. That's who He is. There is no hammer to beat you over the head with for eternity. There is only love.

> *Don't run and hide. There is no hiding, He's everywhere, and He loves you*

It is sin that separates us from Him. It does not separate Him from us, but us from Him.

¹³ You made all the delicate inner parts of my body and knit me together in my mother's womb.

¹⁴ Thank you for making me so wonderfully complex! Your workmanship is marvelous - how well I know it

¹⁵ You watched me as I was being formed in utter seclusion, as I was woven together in the dark of the womb.

> ¹⁶ **You saw me before I was born. Every day of my life was recorded in your book every moment was laid out before a single day had passed.**

You can receive this to be speaking of yourself, which is a great thing to do to help you get a better understanding of how intimately He knows you. He watched you in your mother's womb as you were being formed. Think about that! But in the light of this message of abortion recovery, let's see it as describing the baby. This proves from the very word of God that life and creation begin at the *moment* of conception. Our DNA is created at the *moment of conception.* The color of our eyes, how tall we will be, our frame, the way we fold our hands and cross our legs. Absolutely everything about us is in our DNA and was incepted into us at that moment. The Bible even says that God knows how many hairs are on your head!

> **Mathew 10:30 The very hairs on your head are numbered. (KJV)**

The only difference between a baby you can hold, a child, an adult, or a baby too small to be seen is *time.*

Vs.16 says, He recorded every day of our life in His book. Every moment was laid out before a *single day* had passed. Even if life is only 6-8 weeks long before it is aborted, *that life was recorded in Gods book and is precious to Him.* Just as you are, every life is because HE creates EVERY life. Did you ever stop to think about when your life began? Do you think you weren't really a life until you were 10 weeks old in your mother's womb? When you think of it in terms of yourself, it doesn't even make sense that life isn't a life until it is 10 weeks old does it? Aren't you glad that someone decided you were a life at conception? Your mother gave you a chance to grow into a 9- month old child before God brought you out and breathed His holy breath into your lungs. So, if your life began the moment of conception, likewise your baby was a baby at conception. You *are* a mother or father, and always will be. If you have 5 children born here on earth, you have 6 altogether. If you're like me and have never had children here on earth, you have one in heaven waiting for you to arrive! If you are a man and your spouse or girlfriend had an abortion after getting pregnant with your child, you have a child in heaven. Let me mention here that I am always blessed and surprised at the number of men this message touches. The response from men when I deliver this message is astounding. Many have told me stories of times when they ran into an old girlfriend. The girl told them she had an abortion after they broke up. Or worse, I have heard stories of women aborting a man's child while they were together and not telling them until it was over. Also, many men admitted to funding multiple abortions. All of these men now realize that they have many children in heaven!

> *This proves from the very word of God that life and creation begin at the moment of conception. Our DNA is created at the moment of conception*

Whether your baby was aborted, miscarried or was stillborn, you are the mother or father of that child. Who else would be? And when you get to heaven, you will be reunited with your child or children! Why? Your innocent baby, who never did anything wrong, could not make conscious decisions to sin. Therefore, it is in heaven. And you will see them again. Just like death from miscarriage, death at birth, or death after a long life. It is all the same to God. We are all His creation; His fingerprints are all over us we are so very precious to Him.

> *And when you get to heaven, you will be reunited with your child or children!*

Right now, you may be feeling the weight of your abortion decision, but that's what this message is about. You can turn that guilt and shame into freedom by confessing what you did as sin, admit it was wrong and receiving forgiveness. That pain and heaviness is the Holy Spirit dealing with your sin nature. He is gently revealing and convicting you of your sin. Conviction of the Holy Spirit is to reveal sin in our lives. We then need to confess the sin out to God, repent, receive forgiveness and get back into the wonderful fellowship with God that He desires to have with us. Then you will be free to rejoice at the thought of seeing your children again. This is His plan! Freedom through forgiveness! He knew we were going to blow it, and He gave us His comforter, teacher and guide, the Holy Spirit. Don't be afraid of the pain, it reveals sin, and brings healing. God sent Jesus as an atonement for our sin. Through Him, we can receive forgiveness for our sin, through our repentance.

I always say *don't run from the pain, run to it!* This is God desiring to take you to another level. He is metaphorically peeling off another layer of the onion, revealing more character flaws, sins, unrighteous thinking. He wants us free. He desires to live *in you*, and *with you*, at the deepest level, you can handle. But He can't live in Sin City, so the Holy Spirit shows us what needs to be cleaned out of the house. Then God can freely move within you and not be limited to only the rooms we let Him into. He wants all of you!

Throw open those closet doors. You know, the doors you pray no one ever sees, and they hold your darkest secrets. Those are the things you tell no one but God sees. He knows, was there, and He still loves you. He wants you to confess and allow Him to give you the strength and courage to keep that closet cleaned out with His word and Spirit. There is nothing worth trying to hide from Him. When you see it for what it is you realize how silly it is! We are the only ones that don't see our stuff, bad attitudes, and habits. God and most everyone else can see it all. So, lets clear it out and

Can you see now that not talking about your abortion is hurting you?

be free! Thank God we have a God who is willing to put up with all of this and patiently wait for us. That's how much He so loves us and longs for us.

Can you see now that *not* talking about your abortion is hurting *you*? I believe you know it was wrong because the word says so. The book of Romans states that we all know right from wrong and can hear the truth in our heart.

Romans 1:19 the truth of God is known instinctively, for God has embedded this knowledge inside every human heart. (TPT)

God has written His law on our hearts. It is our natural instinct to know what is right and wrong. And, if you were ok with it, you wouldn't be reading this book of hope and healing for abortion recovery. That's why even though it was legal for you to get an abortion, you knew in your heart it was wrong. *Therein lies the struggle.* Abortion is not ok. It is murder. We don't have the right to kill an innocent child. Abortion is so traumatic that it is now labeled a PTSD (Post Traumatic Stress Disorder). PTSD is defined as a commonly recognized condition that often follows traumatizing events such as witnessing an act of violence or experiencing a natural disaster."

Killing a life is traumatic! Look at all the brave soldiers that come back from their tours, and from the battlefields of war and they can't talk about the lives they have taken. My father was a major in the Air Force. As a Bombardier and Navigator, He flew 48 missions over the Himalayan mountains in WWII. He never spoke about it. As a matter of fact, he would wake up screaming at night when he first got home from that war. You cannot take another human's life and never have repercussions from it. Again, I believe one of the most confusing things about abortion is that its legal. "Why should it bother me if it's ok to do it?" And now your living with all these feelings of guilt, regret, remorse, sadness, depression, and condemnation. Let me show you some PTSD symptoms and see if you relate to any of these:

Patterns of PTSD include:

> Guilt, anxiety, depression, avoiding children or pregnant women, feeling "numb," grief, help-lessness, suicidal thoughts, despair, sorrow, anniversary reminders, fear of infertility, unable to bond with children, lowered self-esteem, dis-trust, hostility, dependency on alcohol/chemicals/ food/work, sexuality problems, self-condemna-tion, weeping, emptiness, distrust, frustration, insomnia, nightmares, dysfunctional rela-tionships, flashbacks, anger, fear of rejection, bitterness, un-forgiveness, fear of commitment, and the inability to form close relationships.

Wow! I couldn't believe it when I first read those symptoms. This answered so many questions for me. How about you? You can't take a life and feel nothing. Even if the abortion wasn't yours, maybe it was a family member, friend, whatever the case, it has touched you, and you need to forgive. We will get to that!

Are you finding it hard to believe that God would forgive you and that He loves you right now? Have you always felt like God has a big hammer and is going to hit you over the head for being such a bad person, a horrible sinner, terrible spouse, friend, sister, on and on, and on…WAIT! Don't give up and don't stop reading. This all gets so much better! Ok, you are still reading, that's good. However, you are wading through the conviction, guilt, shame, and that's why this Psalm is so wonderful. Look what comes next! Though He *knows* what you did. Even though He was there *with you* while you did it, with His heartbreaking, *He still loves you*, aches for you, and can't stop thinking about you. Look what vs. 17 says:

> ¹⁷ **How precious are your thoughts about me O God. They cannot be numbered!**
> ¹⁸ **I can't even count them: they outnumber** *the grains of sand*! **(think about that!) And when I wake up, you are still with me.**

Can you believe that? That is our God. He loved us first in the midst of our sin.

And He not only loves you but is so *IN LOVE* with you that He can't stop thinking about you! Think about someone you love with all your heart. How much do you think about them? Is there someone that you love so much that you think about them all day long? What about your kids?

Think about how much you truly love them. Even when you know this person that you love has done something incredibly wrong, do you love them less? No! You ache for them to make it right and get back into fellowship again. Whether it's with you or someone else, you can see what they're missing! That is such a small, minuscule example of us in our feeble attempt at conditionally loving people. Our God blows all of that away. He loves us so much more than that. Our love is conditional, His is *unconditional.* This person you thought of that you love with all your heart; can you say that your thoughts

> *Our love is conditional, His is unconditional*

about that person outnumber the grains of sand? Probably not. We can't even think that much! However, God can. The Bible says that His thoughts and ways are so much higher than our thoughts and ways:

> **In Isaiah 55:9 God says to us: For as the heavens are higher than the earth, so are my ways higher than your ways, and my thoughts than your thoughts. (NLT)**

Let your heart find hope in the powerful love He has for us. Imagine how much He thinks about you! I'm sure you're a wonderful person, but that's NOT *why* He thinks about you so much. It's not because you were good to your kids today, served faithfully in the kitchen ministry at church, or were especially kind to your mom last week. God isn't, won't, and can't be moved by any of that to love you. He loves you because He IS love. He doesn't act it or feel it, He IS it! It's just how God is! He loves us *completely.* He loves us with our warts, sins and all. He can't ever love us less. It is impossible. It's not in Him to do it. And just as God did with Adam and Eve, I believe He wants to draw us out from hiding so he can cover us *as we confess* to Him what we've done to cause the shame. He wants us to know that it doesn't matter where we hide, he'll be there. Just as He was there when we sinned. He knows. He still loves us just as much as He did before we sinned. Are you beginning to get even a small idea of how much He loves you? You may have never heard it like this before, but it's true. It's in the Bible in black and white!

No, my friend! There is no fist waiting to discipline you or cold shoulder. On the contrary, He is waiting for you to come to him. He has open arms waiting to receive you, pull you into His loving embrace and make everything right again. But...He can't do that until we *repent*.

Sin separates us from Him, not Him from us... but us from Him.

We must confess our sin to Him, repent, and receive forgiveness for our sin. This will be hard, but you must do it. You must see abortion for what it is. Abortion is wrong, it is murder, and the 6th commandment *commands* us not to kill. It is not for us to decide whether

> *Sin separates us from Him, not Him from us... but us from Him*

a life can live. That is for God to choose. Therefore, if you have participated *in any way* in taking the life of your own child, I encourage you to repent and ask for forgiveness from God. *Stop hiding in shame and guilt.* You can see by now that you're not keeping anything in the dark. Remember darkness and light are the same to Him. There is no one else to be concerned about when it comes to your repentance. Your biggest concern should be about what God thinks.

Now hopefully you understand some about how much He loves you. Wonderful isn't it? I invite you to talk to Him right now. Take this moment and confess it out, ask Him to forgive you. He is faithful and just to forgive. Just use your own words and tell Him how you feel, admit the abortion was wrong and ask Him to forgive you.

God doesn't forgive us because we are good, He forgives us because *He* is good.

Then, *receive* His forgiveness. It is a free gift from Him!

He gives His forgiveness freely to us, but it cost Him *everything He had*.

It's not like He gave up the Son He wasn't too crazy about to die for your sin. No! He gave His best, His only, and *beloved* Son for you. So, receive the atonement for your sin. It is so powerful and precious. Then I want you to realize that God needs you! He has so much for you to do! He is there waiting for *you* to make your relationship with Him right again. He longs for

> *God doesn't forgive us because we are good, He forgives us because He is good*

it. He'll do it. His word says in 1 John 1:9 "If we confess our sins to God, He is faithful and just to forgive us our sin." God cannot lie. If He said it, He will do it. If you go to Him with a repentant heart, all will be well, and you will be free from this glass ceiling you have had over your life. Freedom is wonderful!

CHAPTER 6

My Anger is Only Hurting Me

This next section of the Psalm talks about your anger, your relationships and the offenses your holding against others. This also includes the others that were involved in your abortion with you.

¹⁹ O God if only you would destroy the wicked!

How did you get pregnant? Was it a difficult time in your life? A rape, an affair, a man that left you when he found out, your husband, boyfriend, uncle, date rape, incest, prom night? I have heard so many stories and much pain.

Who was the "wicked" in your life? Do you want the wicked destroyed? Are you angry at the people involved? So many different stories: Prom night, it was her first time, she became pregnant, and they decided to abort. 10 years later it is haunting her. She ended up marrying the boy that she got pregnant with! However, she still resents him for that first child they lost. Another woman had an affair in the church. Yes, in the church, sin is everywhere! She got pregnant, the man didn't want his wife to find out, threatened to leave her unless she had an abortion. So, she had one, he paid for it, and he left her anyway. She holds all the guilt shame, anger, hatred, and left the church. Oh, the stories and the pain that drive me to write this book! God sees, He knows, cares and wants us free. But, as verse 19 says, we want the wicked in our lives to pay. We want them destroyed especially if it was a violent sexual act that resulted in pregnancy.

What about the doctors? The abortionists?

vs. 19 continues: Get out of my life you murderers!

Are you angry with the doctor? I was! He was the most rude and uncaring man I had ever experienced. His eyes were cold, dark and completely void of compassion. What was yours like?

Another story is of a young woman who told me her story. She was married and thought she was pregnant. She took a pregnancy test at home, and it appeared to be negative. Then she started bleeding. She went to the doctor for an examination. Upon examination, the doctor told her he thought she needed a procedure to clear her uterus of fibroids. He did not believe she was pregnant. He performed the DNC and found a mass. He removed it and sent it to pathology for testing. He later told her, as she stated "apologizing profusely with tears in his eyes" telling her she was pregnant, and he had removed her baby.

She was angry.

So many stories, so much pain.

> ²⁰ **they blaspheme you: your enemies misuse**
> **your name**
> ²¹ **O Lord, shouldn't I despise those who**
> **oppose you?**
> ²² **Yes, I hate them with total hatred, for your**
> **enemies are my enemies.**

Do you have people in your life who don't love God? Did any of your friends or family encourage you to keep your baby? None of mine did. I resented them for that. *No one* encouraged me to keep my child. I even had a boss who was pregnant at the same time and was *insisting* that I get an abortion with her. She was trying to justify her own abortion by trying to get me to go at the same time. You have to watch out for people who want to keep you down with them. I seriously wonder without her voice in my head *every day*, if I wouldn't have made a different choice with my baby. But in my young mind, I felt I had no choice. I had no family and no support system. I was young, not settled down, still partying, and life was not serious yet! I agreed with her, my friends and

"associations are everything." Your people are your future

the lie they all told me, "Wait until later when I'm married and settled down. You can have kids then." The only thing is, it never happened. I never got pregnant again. I tried for years, nothing. Was that a result of the abortion? Did the "Ice Doctor" damage or perforate my uterus? I'll never know, but I wish I had made better choices in friends. My Pastor has taught us for 35 years that "associations are everything." Your people are your future.

I want to take a moment and talk about relationships in this part. God is saying here that if we love people that are in the world, that is people who do worldly things, things that don't bring God glory, that we are His enemy! Shouldn't we despise those who despise Him? We *are* called to love everyone, but we *don't* need to fellowship with anyone who shakes their fist at God.

> **James 4:4 says: Don't you realize that friendship with the world makes you an enemy of God? I say it again: If you want to be a friend of the world, you make yourself an enemy of God. (NLT)**

We can't have it both ways and be able to walk close with God in peace and freedom. It indeed isn't worth it. I know there may be some relationships that you don't want to leave, but I promise you that walking with God is better than *anything anyone* else could ever do for you. He may be trying to get someone out of your life, let Him! He knows what and who are best for us. Not every relationship is forever. Some are just to help us to the next level. If they don't want to continue with you, let them go!

Jesus said "**I am the true vine and my Father is the Gardner. HE cuts off every branch that doesn't produce fruit, and He will prune the branches that do bear fruit, so they will produce even more!**" John 15:1 (TPT)

Is God in His infinite wisdom trying to cut something out of your life? A relationship that doesn't bear fruit for you or Him? I know in myself there have been people that have left, and I keep trying to graft them back into the vine (me). And God wants them gone from my life! They will not bear good fruit but may bring disease and sickness to the vine (Me). He is cutting off the branches that don't bear fruit. I have learned, and as a matter of fact, now I pray continuously for God to take out of my life who He *doesn't* want in it and bring me to the people who He *wants* in my life. I am very cautious now with whom I give myself to in a friendship/relationship. They must love God first, be an active part of the body of Christ, be generous, happy and going somewhere with their life. They must also be encouraging me in where I'm going with mine! The Bible says we can't walk with God and be a friend of the world too. What are your qualifications for relationship with you? I encourage you to write them down and make sure any new friends are up to your standards. This is making hard, good decisions for your future. Be strong and trust God for your friends. I encourage you to pray this right now:

> *I pray continuously for God to take out of my life who He doesn't want in it and bring me to the people who He wants in my life*

Father, I only want to have in my life those people whom you have chosen for me. Take out of my life anyone who you don't want in it and bring to me those who you do want in my life. I trust you Lord, and give you full reign in all my relationships in Jesus name, Amen.

That is probably one of the very best prayers I have ever prayed. I think my heart was pounding in my chest the first time I prayed it, but over time I have learned to only want in my life who God has for me. You'll be shocked at who will leave your life, and you'll be blessed abundantly by who He adds to you as you grow in Him. Very good for you for praying that prayer. When you see what God does, and when you LET Him do what He knows is best, you will be like me and pray that all the time. You can do this! You are strong and courageous and going after the things of God!

CHAPTER 7

His Forgiveness Heals Me

²³ Search me, O God, and know my heart: test
me and know my anxious thoughts.
²⁴ Point out anything in me that offends you
and lead me along the path of everlasting
life.

In this last part, God wants us to see that you cannot live with anger, hatred, shame, and guilt of your abortion or any other sin in your hearts. These things hold us back, make us bitter and resentful and generally unhappy people. (I also believe holding all of that inside opens the door to sickness and disease.) I have heard many women state how they used to be so happy and full of life. However, now because of the shame of their abortion, they can't live free. That statement is not true and is the reason for this beautiful message from your Heavenly Father! By asking Him to search us, we allow Him to show us the things we can't see. It's the age-old saying, "There are three sides to me, the one I see, the one I allow others to see, and the one I can't see. I add to that the fourth side: the side God sees. That is the side we should be most concerned about. So here we need to ask God to show us what we can't see. We need to get right with Him. He wants us to pray these last 2 verses as a prayer. "Search me and know my mind, my will, my emotions oh God. Is there anything there that offends you?" "Test me and know my anxious thoughts."

> *There are three sides to me, the one I see, the one I allow others to see, and the one I can't see. I add to that the fourth side: the side God sees*

Why would your thoughts be anxious? Fear. You're trying to hang onto something that He wants you to let go of. Anxiety is rooted in fear. Fear is self-serving, and it is not from God. It is being afraid that you won't get what *you think* you want. Time to change your thinking. Give your anxious thoughts over to peace. Trust God while letting Him be the Master Gardner. He will only do what the very best thing for us is, and ultimately what will make us completely fulfilled. He only wants us to be happy. He loves us! Ask Him to know you, and test you. This *invites* Him to teach you how to be more like Him. To learn how to walk in the fruit of who He is. Galatians 5:22 says the fruit of God's spirit is: "Love, Joy, Peace, Patience, kindness, goodness, gentleness, humility and self-control." These are who God is. This is what He desires for us to have every moment of every day. Can you imagine living in those things continually? You can! You just need to make room in your heart by getting rid of what doesn't serve Him, or you. That is to say, what offends Him.

Vs. 24: Point out anything in me that offends you, and then lead me on your path.

Unforgiveness offends God. Forgiveness is what He came to earth for. We *must* forgive. This is the key to it all. Forgive those who hurt you, left you, abused you, lied to you, used you, betrayed you, raped you or abandoned you. Whatever the offense is against someone else, you *must* forgive them in your heart. I know this sounds difficult for certain circumstances, even impossible, but it is the way out. This is the way to break that glass ceiling that has been over your life all this time. *Forgive. You must.* Just as Jesus forgave you, freely, you must forgive. It is the way to freedom. Your standing in unforgiveness is a self-righteous way of thinking. I know it seems justified. Your circumstances may be horrible! But that doesn't lessen the price of the blood that was shed for their sin as well as yours. They are forgiven by God, and so are you.

> *holding offense against someone is like you drinking the poison and waiting for the other person to die*

Judgement is *God's*. *He* will repay. Everyone must answer for their sins. Let unforgiveness not be one of yours. Let it go and be free! It is said that *holding offense against someone is like you*

42

drinking the poison and waiting for the other person to die. You're not hurting anyone with your anger and bitterness. It only hurts *you. Forgive.* Whoever, whatever, however. You must. You may want to write a letter to the person/people who were involved, and then imagine them in a chair in front of you and read it to them! (I would not suggest doing this in person.) Then you can tear the letter up, burn it, shred it, whatever you want to do with it but let it be done and gone! I did this, and it is powerful. I didn't realize how much anger I still had inside of me until I wrote the letters and delivered them to my imaginary people in chairs. Let me just say I had a few to write, but that is another book!

Here is something I must include: Maybe you said you couldn't afford to have a child. Let me share this with you.

> Isaiah 46:3-5 "Listen to me, descendants of Jacob, all you who remain in Israel. I have cared for you since you were born. Yes, I carried you *before you were born.* ⁴ I will be your God throughout your lifetime— until your hair is white with age. I made you, and I will care for you. I will carry you along and save you. ⁵ "To whom will you compare me? Who is my equal? (NLT)

God's plan was to carry us and care for us our entire life until our hair was white with age. It is not our place to terminate a life because *we* can't afford to take care of it. He will care for us and provide for us. He loves us so!

But please remember, in most cases your abortion is just that, *YOUR* abortion. *I* decided to have mine. Even in all my circumstances, the blame still lies with *me*. I got on the table alone. I had to forgive myself, and so do you. First, understand the abortion was *wrong*. So very, very wrong. I will not sugarcoat it. It was. Own it, sincerely repent of it, asking God to forgive you. I understand there are circumstances, I have heard so many stories, but the bottom line is YOU got on the table. In most cases, people willingly paid for the abortion. We must see it as it is. Remember, God sees in the dark, He knows. There is no point in hiding. You can even ask your baby to forgive you. I don't know if our children in heaven can hear us, but it may help *you* to ask.

> *I had to forgive myself, and so do you*

Then *receive* the forgiveness. Hallelujah! God who is so rich in mercy and grace will forgive if you ask. And then, its over! Not only will He forgive it, but He will also forget it! The Bible says in

Psalm 103:12 He has removed our sins as far from us as the east is from the west. (NLT)

And in Isaiah 1:18 says: Come, let's talk this over, says the Lord; no matter how deep the stain of your sins, I can take it out and make you as clean as freshly fallen snow. Even if you are stained as red as crimson, I can make you white as wool! (NLT)

I want you to pause a moment and think about that. He REMOVES our sin. It's gone! No more! When you see Him in heaven and want to ask for His forgiveness for this, He literally won't know what you're talking about! That's the power of the blood of our Savior Jesus. His blood atoned for all our sin. That is how I can travel and give this message to anyone who will listen and look them in the eye and tell them they can be forgiven as I am with my head held high! Certainly not because of anything I've done. We've seen what a mess I made but stood strong because of this wonderful atoning blood, and the forgiveness of my Father God. He is so faithful to forgive because of His love for us. His love is higher, deeper, wider and longer than we could ever realize or understand because we don't love as He does. Our love is conditional, and His love never is! He loves everyone unconditionally, no matter what they have done!

Remember: He doesn't forgive us because we are good, He forgives us because *HE is good.*

I am free from the sin of abortion because I saw it as sin, and I confessed it out to God and received His forgiveness for my sin. Hear me, as I have said, *this was the worst mistake I have ever made in my life.* That was the only child I ever would have had. But I know I am forgiven, and I am free. Free to worship, laugh, live, and to find the path God has for me and the thing He has planned for my life. I am free from the guilt and shame that used to cover me like a shroud. I am free to travel far and wide to spread this message. His message of love, forgiveness, and healing from abortion.

My prayer for you is that you receive this message of love and forgiveness from your loving Heavenly Father. I believe with all my heart God sent this message to you. It's no mistake that you're reading this book. Search your heart and find the courage to step into the light of His love and forgiveness.

If you feel that you would like a more in-depth study of this message and Psalm I have written a *10-week study guide* to be used in a small group study. Great healing and freedom can come from a small group support study where you can share with others your story and experiences, and in return hear from them their struggles as well.

Your heavenly Father loves you so dearly. He is there, waiting for you with open, loving arms. Reach out to Him. I promise you will never be the same.

All my love,

Lorna

On the following pages are scriptures about: Your righteousness, God's Love, and Forgiveness. I encourage you to read these every day, speak them out loud about yourself and memorize them! The Word of God brings healing. God bless you. Xoxo

Note* My husband and I are ministry leaders of a Celebrate Recovery™ Group in our church. We truly believe in this ministry. It is a wonderful Christ-centered ministry where you can explore recovery from any hurt, hang-up or habit. In CR you will find love and acceptance without judgement. We are all working on something. I was able to work through deeper aspects of forgiveness regarding my abortion in Celebrate Recovery™, and I believe it prepared me to be able to share this message openly and embrace the freedom I found in Jesus Christ, my savior. I encourage everyone to attend Celebrate Recovery™.

Celebrate Recovery™ is a worldwide ministry. To find a group in your area go to: *www.celebraterecovery.com*

Scriptures

RIGHTEOUSNESS

2 Corinthians 5:17 TPT

Now, if anyone is enfolded into Christ, he has become an entirely new person. All that is related to the old order has vanished. Behold, everything is fresh and new.

2 Corinthians 5:21 TPT

For God made the only one who did not know sin to become sin for us, so that we who did not know righteousness might become the righteousness of God through our union with him.

2 Corinthians 5:7 NLT

For we live by believing and not by seeing.

Philippians 4:13 NLT

For I can do everything through Christ, who gives me strength.

Romans 8:1 NLT

So now there is no condemnation for those who belong to Christ Jesus.

Colossians 1:22 NLT

Yet now he has reconciled you to himself through the death of Christ in his physical body. As a result, he has brought you into his own presence, and you are holy and blameless as you stand before him without a single fault.

Psalms 23:3 KJV

He restoreth my soul: he leadeth me in the paths of righteousness for his name's sake.

Philippians 4:8 NLT

And now, dear brothers and sisters, one final thing. Fix your thoughts on what is true, and honorable, and right, and pure, and lovely, and admirable. Think about things that are excellent and worthy of praise. 9 Keep putting into practice all you learned and received from me—everything you heard from me and saw me doing. Then the God of peace will be with you.

Romans 8:37 NLT

Despite all these things, overwhelming victory is ours through Christ, who loved us.

Ecclesiastes 5:20 NLT

God keeps such people so busy enjoying life that they take no time to brood over the past.

Romans 12:1,2 NLT

[1]And so, dear brothers and sisters, I plead with you to give your bodies to God because of all he has done for you. Let them be a living and holy sacrifice—the kind he will find acceptable. This is truly the way to worship him. [2] Don't copy the behavior and customs of this world, but let God transform you into a new person by changing the way you think. Then you will learn to know God's will for you, which is good and pleasing and perfect.

John 8:36 NIV

So if the Son sets you free, you will be free indeed.

Romans 5:1 NLT

Therefore, since we have been made right in God's sight by faith, we have peace with God because of what Jesus Christ our Lord has done for us. [2] Because of our faith, Christ has brought us into this place of undeserved privilege where we now stand, and we confidently and joyfully look forward to sharing God's glory. [3] We can rejoice, too, when we run into problems and trials, for we know that they help us develop endurance. [4] And endurance develops strength of character, and character strengthens our confident hope of salvation.

Galatians 2:20 NLT

My old self has been crucified with Christ. It is no longer I who live, but Christ lives in me. So, I live in this earthly body by trusting in the Son of God, who loved me and gave himself for me.

Joshua 1:9 NLT

This is my command—be strong and courageous! Do not be afraid or discouraged. For the LORD, your God is with you wherever you go."

Ephesians 6:10 NLT

A final word: Be strong in the Lord and in his mighty power.

"I am who God says I am, I can do what God says I can do I will be what God says I can be!"

FORGIVENESS

Psalm 103:12 NLT

He has removed our sins as far from us as the east is from the west.

Isaiah 1:18 NLT

"Come now, let's settle this," says the LORD. "Though your sins are like scarlet, I will make them as white as snow. Though they are red like crimson, I will make them as white as wool.

Psalm 86:15 TPT

But you, O Lord, are a God of compassion and mercy, slow to get angry and filled with unfailing love and faithfulness.

Psalm 103:3 TPT

He forgives all my sins and heals all my diseases.

1 John 1:9 TPT

But if we confess our sins to him, he is faithful and just to forgive us our sins and to cleanse us from all wickedness.

John 3:17 TPT

God sent his Son into the world not to judge the world, but to save the world through him.

Romans 8:38-39 TPT

[38]So now I live with the confidence that there is nothing in the universe with the power to separate us from God's love. I'm convinced that his love will triumph over death, life's troubles, fallen angels, or dark rulers in the heavens. There is nothing in our present or future circumstances that can weaken his love. [39]There is no power above us or beneath us—no power that could ever be found in the universe that can distance us from God's passionate love, which is lavished upon us through our Lord Jesus, the Anointed One!

Lamentations 3:22-23 NLT

Great is his faithfulness: his mercies begin afresh each morning. I say to myself, "The LORD is my inheritance; therefore, I will hope in him!"

1 John 3:16 TPT

This is how we have discovered love's reality: Jesus sacrificed his life for us. Because of this great love, we should be willing to lay down our lives for one another.

GOD'S LOVE

Jeremiah 31:3 NLT

"I have loved you, my people, with an everlasting love. With unfailing love, I have drawn you to myself".

John 16:27 TPT

For the Father tenderly loves you, because you love me and believe that I've come from God.

John 3:16 TPT

For this is how much God loved the world—He gave His one and only, unique Son as a gift. So now everyone who believes in him will never perish but experience everlasting life.

Psalm 139:17 TPT

Every single moment you are thinking of me! How precious and wonderful to consider that you cherish me constantly in your every thought!

Jeremiah 29:11 NLT

"For I know the plans I have for you," says the LORD. "They are plans for good and not for disaster, to give you a future and a hope."

2 Thessalonians 2:16-17 NLT

Now may our Lord Jesus Christ himself and God our Father, who loved us and by his grace gave us eternal comfort and a wonderful hope, [17] comfort you and strengthen you in every good thing you do and say.

Psalm 23:6 TPT

So why would I fear the future? For your goodness and love pursue me all the days of my life. Then afterward, when my life is through, I'll return to your glorious presence to be forever with you!

Psalm 34:18 TPT

The Lord is close to all whose hearts are crushed by pain, and he is always ready to restore the repentant one.

Romans 8:35 TPT

Who could ever separate us from the endless love of God's Anointed One? *Absolutely no one!* For nothing in the universe has the power to diminish his love toward us. Troubles, pressures, and problems are unable to come between us and heaven's love. What about persecutions, deprivations, dangers, and death threats? No, for they are all impotent to hinder omnipotent love.

Romans 8:38 TPT

So now I live with the confidence that there is nothing in the universe with the power to separate us from God's love. I'm convinced that his love will triumph over death, life's troubles, fallen angels, or dark rulers in the heavens. There is nothing in our present or future circumstances that can weaken his love. [39] There is no power above us or beneath us—no power that could ever be found in the universe that can distance us from God's passionate love, which is lavished upon us through our Lord Jesus, the Anointed One!

Prayer for Serenity

God, grant me the serenity
to accept the things I cannot change,
the courage to change the things I can,
and the wisdom to know the difference.
Living one day at a time,
enjoying one moment at a time;
accepting hardship as a pathway to peace;
taking, as Jesus did,
this sinful world as it is,
not as I would have it;
trusting that You will make all things right
if I surrender to Your will;
so that I may be reasonable happy in this life
and supremely happy with You forever in the next.

Amen.
Reinhold Niebuhr

Made in the USA
Columbia, SC
19 April 2019